What is an Anabaptist Christian?

Palmer Becker

Introduction

Anabaptist-minded Christians have existed from the very beginning of the Christian era. In nearly every group of churches and perhaps in nearly every congregation, there are people who have an Anabaptist understanding of the Christian faith. Anabaptist is a way of being Christian. Just as there are Anglican, Baptist or Charismatic Christians, so there are Anabaptist Christians.

"Anabaptist" is an invented name meaning "re-baptizers." It was given to Christians who, during the 16th-century Reformation, rejected infant baptism, and instead baptized each other as adults upon confession of faith. Anabaptists were the forerunners of the Free Church tradition, which included the Mennonites.

Anabaptist/Mennonite Christians hold many beliefs in common with other believers. They believe in a personal three-in-one God who is both holy and gracious, in salvation by grace through repentance and faith, in the humanity and divinity of Jesus, in the inspiration and authority of Scripture, in the power of the Holy Spirit, and in the church as the body of Christ. But they hold these convictions somewhat differently than many.

Anabaptists are sometimes identified as the third wing of the Great Reformation. They rose up in a time of social upheaval and were intent on completing the reformation begun by Martin Luther, Ulrich Zwingli and John Calvin. In general, Anabaptist-minded Christians place a greater emphasis than most on following Jesus in daily life, being part of a Christ-centered community, and seeking to overcome conflict in nonviolent ways. Are you an Anabaptist-minded Christian?

Martin Luther brought us to the clear understanding that salvation comes by grace through faith, but too often he made the mistake of going back only to the structures and thinking set in motion by Constantine and Augustine. Mennonite Christians have sometimes made a similar mistake by going back only to what was set in motion by Menno Simons and the 16th-century Anabaptists. All Christians need to pause at the 16th century to observe what it meant to be a Christian in that time and culture, but then they need to go all the way back to Jesus, the author and founder of our faith, to explore what it means to be a Christian in our time.

In his book, *Differentiate or Die*, Jack Trout says that it is essential for individuals and organizations to distinguish themselves from each other. "If an organization does not have something unique to offer," says Trout, "it will die."[1] A similar article published in the *Harvard Business Review* says that the unique core values that brought an organization into being are "sacred" and should not be changed.[2]

What are the "sacred" core values of Anabaptist Christians? This booklet will explain them in the form of three key statements that profoundly affect our believing, belonging and behaving.[3] They are:

1. ***Jesus* is the center of our faith.**
2. ***Community* is the center of our lives.**
3. ***Reconciliation* is the center of our work.**

The three statements of this booklet are a modern-day adaptation of *The Anabaptist Vision*, an articulate and widely accepted statement made in 1943 by Harold S. Bender, president of the American Society of Church History.[4] Bender explains from his understanding of Scripture that:

1. Christianity is *discipleship*. It is following *Jesus* in everyday life.
2. The Church is a *brotherhood* or *family*. Members not only commit themselves to Christ, but also individually and voluntarily to each other.
3. Followers of Jesus have an *ethic of love and nonresistance*. As transformed persons, they seek to be reconcilers who reject involvement in violence and warfare.

This booklet will describe how these core values developed in history, and suggest how they apply to today's world. It will then present them in contrasting statements with questions for discussion. Its purpose is to give inquiring persons an opportunity to ask and at least partially answer the question, "Am I an Anabaptist-minded Christian?"

I wish to express special appreciation to Jeff Wright, conference minister for the Pacific Southwest Mennonite Conference, who sparked the imagination for this work. I am also grateful for the theologically diverse members of Americus (Ga.) Mennonite Fellowship; my brother-in-law, Theodore A. Weathers; and other readers who vigorously critiqued the initial drafts of this paper. I take responsibility for its content, recognizing that for study purposes I have emphasized the positive contributions of the early Anabaptists and minimized the negatives. Many evangelicals may well find themselves somewhere between the positions that I have described.

Core Value #1: Jesus is the center of our faith

Jesus

Jesus began his ministry in approximately 30 CE by gathering together a group of disciples. For three years these disciples lived, ate and worked together with Jesus. They observed him as he cared for the poor, healed those who were ill, gave sight to the blind, and taught the multitudes. During these years, and also in the days after his resurrection, he became central to their lives and faith. They became believers who accepted him as their Master-Teacher, Savior and Lord.

However, to be a Christian meant more to them than being a believer or worshiper. It meant being a disciple or a follower of Jesus who was filled with the spirit of Jesus. Because of this, they became Christ-like in their lifestyles. If you had asked those first disciples, I believe they would have said with enthusiasm, "*Jesus is the center of our faith!*"

For 250 years these early believers focused on the life, ministry, death and resurrection of Jesus. But then two men arose who set in motion so many changes to the core values of the Christian faith that it nearly became another religion.[5] One was a politician. The other was a theologian.

Constantine

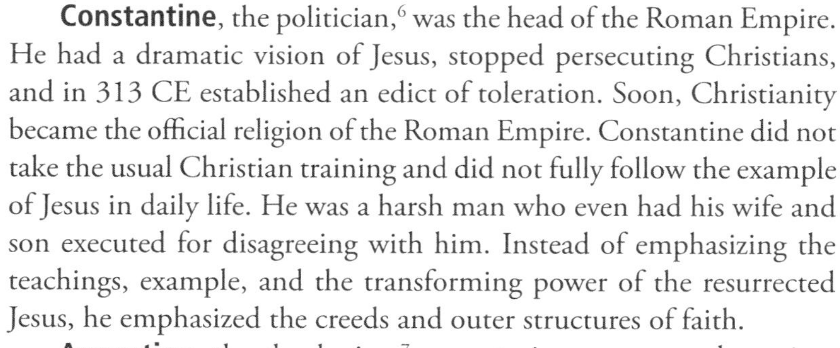

Constantine, the politician,[6] was the head of the Roman Empire. He had a dramatic vision of Jesus, stopped persecuting Christians, and in 313 CE established an edict of toleration. Soon, Christianity became the official religion of the Roman Empire. Constantine did not take the usual Christian training and did not fully follow the example of Jesus in daily life. He was a harsh man who even had his wife and son executed for disagreeing with him. Instead of emphasizing the teachings, example, and the transforming power of the resurrected Jesus, he emphasized the creeds and outer structures of faith.

Augustine

Augustine, the theologian,[7] came to importance a short time later. Some would call him the greatest theologian of the early church. But he, too, had a different perspective on Jesus and the Christian faith than did the first disciples. Instead of focusing on Christ's life and ministry, Augustine and his followers focused on his death. The Apostles' Creed, which developed during this time, omits the teaching and ministry of Jesus. Instead of saying, "*Jesus* is the center of our faith," Augustine and his followers tended to say, "*Christ's death* is the center of our faith."

People began believing that infants are born sinners, that humans can do no good, and that God decides if they are going to heaven or to hell. Trust in the sacraments or rituals of the church became central. For a thousand years, many of the priests, bishops and popes of the church focused on the death of Christ without a proper focus on his life, teachings and Holy Spirit presence. As a result, morality fell to a very low level.

Martin Luther

Between the years 1200 and 1500 CE, a variety of concerned persons began to realize that there was something seriously wrong with the church's understanding of salvation and the body of Christ. **Martin Luther**, a German monk, who was thoroughly schooled in Augustinian theology, was one of these. Ulrich Zwingli, a Swiss pastor, was another. They came forward to introduce reform.

Luther was especially offended by the practices of priests and popes who offered forgiveness and deliverance from purgatory on the basis of works and by selling indulgences. On October 31, 1517, with a desire to call for public debate on the nature of the Christian faith, he nailed a list of 95 theses, or arguments, to the church door in Wittenberg, Germany. This nailing of these theses launched the Great Reformation.[8]

At first, Luther and Zwingli saw the church as a gathering of mature believers who were committed both to Christ and to each other. They affirmed the Scriptures as their sole authority for faith and practice, and insisted that salvation is by the grace of God. Unfortunately, their view of salvation was largely limited to receiving eternal life through forgiveness and being justified before a holy, demanding God. It had little to do with believing in a new way of life or of belonging to each other in community.

Several students of Ulrich Zwingli, including Conrad Grebel, Felix Manz and George Blaurock, came together for regular Bible study in Zurich, Switzerland. Hans Hut, Hans Denck and Pilgram Marpeck were on a similar pilgrimage in South Germany. Somewhat later, **Menno Simons**, a transformed Catholic priest, helped coordinate groups that were emerging in Holland.[9]

Menno Simons

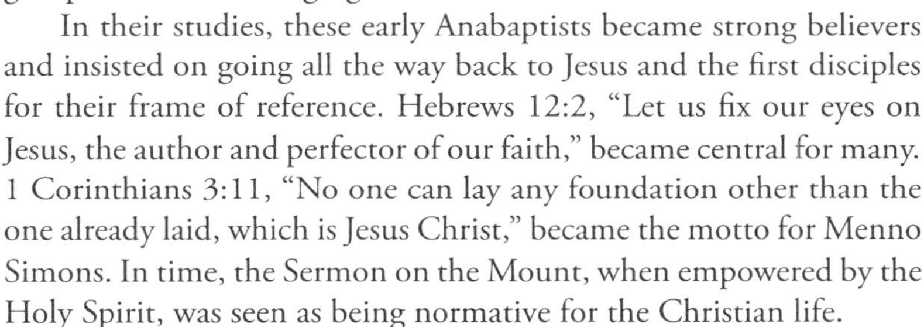

In their studies, these early Anabaptists became strong believers and insisted on going all the way back to Jesus and the first disciples for their frame of reference. Hebrews 12:2, "Let us fix our eyes on Jesus, the author and perfector of our faith," became central for many. 1 Corinthians 3:11, "No one can lay any foundation other than the one already laid, which is Jesus Christ," became the motto for Menno Simons. In time, the Sermon on the Mount, when empowered by the Holy Spirit, was seen as being normative for the Christian life.

While the Anabaptist Christians affirmed the Apostles' Creed and much of what Luther and Zwingli were preaching, they went further in some of their interpretations. They preferred to talk about being "born again" rather than "justified by faith." While salvation was by the grace of God, they believed it called for a response of obedience to Jesus Christ. They insisted that salvation, made possible by the power of the Holy Spirit, leads to the transformation of a person's moral, social and economic life. If you had asked those first Anabaptist Christians, I believe that they would have said with the first disciples, "*Jesus is the center of our faith!*"

Current Anabaptist-minded Christians often seek to apply the 16th-century Anabaptist understandings of Jesus to their everyday lives in at least three important ways:

1. Jesus needs to be followed in daily life

To an Anabaptist Christian, believing means more than affirming a creed or being justified by faith. To be Christian means to be empowered by the Holy Spirit to follow Jesus in daily life. Christianity is discipleship! In German it is called *Nachfolge Christi* or "following after Christ." Anabaptists affirm the statement of Hans Denck, a 16th-century leader, who said, "No one can truly know Christ unless he follows after him in daily life."[10]

Unfortunately, many Christians, even after salvation, still, like Luther, see themselves as hopeless sinners who are unable to live a changed life. Some say, "I'm not different. I am only forgiven." They assume that in salvation the attitude of God toward them changes even if their own attitudes in life have not been significantly changed. For Anabaptist Christians, salvation means turning from an old way of life and walking with Jesus. Since they have been transformed in thought, attitude and action, they will behave differently in relationship to God, to each other, and even to their enemies.

As they celebrate communion, many Anabaptist-minded Christians emphasize that Jesus not only died in their place, but now lives in their midst as an example. They believe that Christ's death and resurrection represent the ultimate expression of God's love, and make it possible for followers of Jesus to overcome the powers of evil. Together with the first disciples and the early Anabaptists, we are challenged to say that the living "*Jesus is the center of our faith!*"

2. The Bible needs to be interpreted from a Christ-centered point of view

Many Christians today have what is called a "flat" Bible. They assume that the words of God interpreted by Moses in the Old Testament are as authorative as the words of Jesus in the New Testament. People with this understanding of Scripture downgrade the importance of Christ's life and words. They often go primarily to the Old Testament for their political and social ethics and to the Ten Commandments for their personal ethics. This way of seeing the Bible determines their stance on such issues as war, capital punishment and social justice.

Other Christians interpret the Scriptures from a dispensational point of view. To know God's will they need to know for which dispensation or period of time a biblical passage was revealed. Unfortunately, this approach generally postpones obedience to the teachings of Jesus in the Sermon on the Mount and other passages until Christ's second coming. During the present time, Jesus receives their worship but not their daily obedience.

From the early Anabaptists we can learn that the Scriptures need to be interpreted from a Christ-centered point of view. All Scripture is to be read and interpreted in the spirit of Jesus. This means that sometimes the teachings of Jesus transcend previous teachings. Jesus himself said, "You have heard it said … but I say to you." Also, the writer of Hebrews says, "In the past, God spoke to our forefathers through the prophets at many times and in various ways, but in these last days, he has spoken to us by his Son … who is the radiance of God's glory and the exact representation of his being …."

Anabaptist-minded Christians are not strict literalists. They seek to interpret all Scripture in the spirit of Jesus. The written word and the spirit of Jesus must be held in creative tension. Christians get into trouble when they either elevate *the written word* over the Spirit or raise *the Spirit* above the word. Word and Spirit need to be held together.[11]

Jesus is Lord over the Scriptures. While the Scriptures are seen as the ultimate source of information, Jesus is nonetheless the fullest revelation of God and the ultimate authority for daily living. Because of this understanding, Anabaptist Christians get their primary guidance and ethics from Jesus rather than from Old Testament codes of law. Missionary Peter Kehler once said, "If all the Scriptures do is introduce me to Jesus Christ, that is enough!"[12]

When we have an ethical question, be it personal, social or political, we need to go first to the words and spirit of Jesus for our guidance and then to other Scriptures for further background and understanding. If two passages of Scripture seem to disagree, let Jesus be the referee!

3. Jesus needs to be accepted as both Savior and Lord

Many Christians affirm Jesus as their eternal Savior, but are weak on seeing him as their daily Lord. As a result, they give their daily obedience to an employer, civic leader, military general or president. While Constantine, Augustine and Luther emphasized salvation through faith in Christ, they too often accepted the government as the final authority or lord in matters of daily life. Many Christians today are more obedient to the commands of earthly leaders than they are to those given by Jesus as interpreted in the body of Christ.

Both the kingdom of God and the kingdoms of this world demand our ultimate obedience. God has ordained government to control evil and to do good in a secular world. We need to obey government to the extent that Christian discipleship permits, but when there is a conflict between the ways of Jesus and the ways of Caesar, we need to say with the early disciples, "We must obey God rather than any human authority."[13]

While we are to obey government, this does not mean giving blind obedience to whatever it commands. Since our highest loyalty always belongs to Jesus Christ, we may on occasion need to disobey a government order because it is contrary to the teaching and spirit of Jesus. When we disobey, we will need to be submissive to the punishments of government. True Anabaptist Christians:

1. Follow Jesus in daily life.
2. Interpret the Scriptures in the spirit of Jesus.
3. Promise their highest loyalty to Jesus Christ.

Jesus is at the center of their faith. Are you an Anabaptist Christian?

Core Value #2: Community is the center of our lives

Jesus

Jesus wanted his followers to not only *believe* in him, but to also have a strong sense of *belonging*. One of the first things that Jesus did when he began his ministry was to form a community. He invited Peter and Andrew and then James and John to join him. Soon, there were many followers from whom he chose 12 disciples. They learned, ate, traveled and served together until at Pentecost they became the core of a new society called the church. The first believers "met day-by-day," not only "in the Temple" (the gathering of the whole church) but "in their homes" (the home congregations or small groups), "eating with glad and humble hearts, praising God, and enjoying the good will of the people" (Acts 2:46-47).

The New Testament church functioned as a fellowship within this dual context. Major teaching and worship were done in the large church context, while in the home groups they studied, prayed and worked together in close fellowship.

Observers were amazed at what God did in and through these people who met not only in the large setting, but also in close-knit, Spirit-filled community. If you would have asked those first followers of Jesus, I believe they would have said, "*Christ-centered community is the center of our lives!*"

Unfortunately, with the coming of **Constantine** and Augustine, the nature of the church changed. Instead of stressing the church as a family of brothers and sisters meeting for Bible study, sharing and prayer, Constantine emphasized only the large church with its buildings and organization. Just as the Romans had built shrines to their gods, so Constantine, with the encouragement and help of his mother, built cathedrals that were similar to shrines on the sites where Jesus had lived or ministered. Eventually, this structural concept of the church spread and a huge cathedral was built in the center of nearly every province of Europe.

Constantine

Augustine and his followers believed that it was not possible to clearly distinguish those who belonged to the body of Christ from those who did not. "The wheat and the weeds grow together," he said. Also, instead of emphasizing the people as the body of Christ, he emphasized the bread and wine of the mass as the body of Christ. As a result, participating in the mass in the large church context became the central experience of the church.

Augustine

A sacramental faith developed. To be cleansed of original sin, one needed the sacrament of baptism. To be forgiven of ongoing sin, believers needed the mass. To be released from purgatory, one needed to buy grants from the pope and to pray to the saints.

The idea of belonging to Christ and to each other in small group community was largely lost. Instead of the church being a counterculture in the world, it became very much like the world. Instead of serving as pastors to a community of believers, the clergy often served as chaplains and advocates of the government. Those who wanted to follow Jesus in daily life and to live in community became monks and nuns. Since these were primarily confined to monasteries and convents, it gave the impression that believing in Jesus and belonging to a community in daily life was impossible for common people.

Martin Luther and other reformers originally intended to reform the church to its biblical basis. They separated themselves from the dictatorial powers of Rome and wanted to become a free church. They taught adult baptism and the priesthood of all believers. However, upon gaining freedom from Rome, many followers of Luther and Zwingli became eager to also be free from the cruel feudal systems of that time. Chaos broke out and ushered in the Peasants' War in which more than 100,000 people died. In an effort to restore order, Luther and Zwingli sided with the rulers and in doing so lost the confidence of many peasants.

Martin Luther

Due to the Peasants' War and other problems, Luther and Zwingli were not able to follow through on their intended reforms. Eventually, they went back only to Constantine for their structures and to Augustine in their theology. This meant returning to the state church as the polity of the church, to the "cathedral" as the structure of the church, to infant baptism as the introductory rite into the church, and to the use of the sword by the government as the tool for discipline. In theology, they continued in the Augustinian tradition of viewing humans through the eyes of being sinners at birth, being unable to overcome sin, and being pre-assigned to heaven or hell by God. Much of Christendom has followed this tradition into the present time.

Menno Simons

Early Anabaptists, including **Menno Simons**, were disappointed that Luther and Zwingli were not following through on their original visions of an independent church composed of transformed believers. They did not merely want to reform the church back to the politics set in motion by Constantine and the theology set in motion by Augustine; they wanted to restore the church all the way back to the New Testament!

Due to persecution, the early Anabaptist Christians met in homes for Bible study, sharing and prayer. Like the early Christians, they experienced Christ in their midst and took communion together with glad and sincere hearts. As people believed in Jesus as their teacher, Savior and Lord, they were baptized and received into a specific congregation where they had a strong sense of belonging.

In contrast to other reformers, Anabaptist Christians spoke of power to live differently rather than merely being free from guilt. Forgiveness was not only removing the walls between themselves and God, but also removing the walls between each other. Eating the Lord's Supper together was a fellowship experience made possible by the forgiveness that they had received from God and each other.

While Luther opposed any and all notions of sainthood, the early Anabaptists expected a "saintly life" from all their members and especially from their leaders. They believed that faithful Christians were transformed people who had repented of their sins and were living high ethical lives. A transformed life was the measure of salvation and Holy Spirit presence. If someone was no longer following Jesus in daily life and was persisting in non-Christ-like living, it was believed that they had voided their commitments and were, therefore, excommunicated from the body of Christ.

Early Anabaptists studied the Scriptures on their own and then came together in small groups where they, with the awareness of the Spirit's presence, gave and received counsel to each other. In these small, Spirit-filled Bible study groups, they confronted each other and thereby made each other strong enough to confront the world.

The Anabaptist view of salvation and the church was seen as very deviant. Many leaders were imprisoned and severely persecuted. More than 4,000 believers were drowned, beheaded, burned at the stake, and in other ways killed as martyrs for their faith.[14]

In the early years, there was much diversity among the Anabaptists. Some leaders were overly concerned about the end times. Others began using violence. A group in Münster, Germany, went so far as to replace the elected city council with 12 elders who introduced polygamy, circulated new currency, and declared themselves to be the New Israel. This minority emphasis, which came to a tragic and bloody end, placed a negative reputation upon Anabaptist and Mennonite Christians that in some circles has lasted until the present time.

People were amazed at how Anabaptist Christians related to each other and then to the world. Their sense of belonging to Jesus and their strong support of each other helped them to live as devoted, ethical, alternative communities in a hostile world. If you would have asked those early Anabaptist Christians, I believe they would have said with the first disciples, "*Christ-centered community is the center of our lives!*"

Current Anabaptist-minded Christians understand and practice Christ-centered community in three rather distinct ways:

1. Forgiveness is seen and practiced as a means toward community

Our three-in-one God who lives in community wants us to also experience the joys of community. Jesus came that we might have life and have it more abundantly. This happens when we are reconciled to God and to each other. To enjoy a warm sense of community and all the benefits pertaining to it, we need to maintain a regular practice of repentance and forgiveness in the body of Christ.

The central problem of humanity is not the lack of finances, the lack of education, or the lack of power. The central problem is that we offend each other. From the very beginning of time, human beings, both as individuals and as groups, have offended God and each other through arrogance, self-centeredness and disobedience. Our offensive attitudes and actions break our relationships with God, with each other, with our inner selves, and with the whole earth. How shall this problem be addressed?

Forgiveness is not only necessary for being reconciled to God; it is also necessary within a reconciled community. The turning point in resolving an offense usually comes when one party sincerely repents and asks for forgiveness. Confession and forgiveness remove the barriers that prevent fellowship with God and each other. Christ's greatest desire is that we be in harmony with each other even as Christ is in harmony with the Father.

Unfortunately, in the non-Christian world, confession and forgiveness are largely neglected. Too often, denial and defensiveness take the place of honest confession. Attempts are made to *forget* without *forgiving*.

2. The Scriptures need to be interpreted in community

Many Christians see trained pastors, priests or instructors as being the only ones who are capable of properly interpreting the Scriptures. All too often, this leaves common members uninvolved in study and application.

Other Christians try to interpret the Scriptures on their own. Unfortunately, when individuals interpret Scripture privately, even with the presence of the Holy Spirit, they too often come up with confusing and false understandings.

Anabaptist-minded Christians believe that the Scriptures need to be studied both individually and together in Spirit-guided community. Scripture passages become clearer and more applicable as we study them with each other in small groups, classes and conferences.

3. The church must be structured for community

The church has sometimes been described as a two-winged bird. One wing is the large, corporate congregation where vertical relationships with our transcendent, holy God are emphasized. The other wing is the small group where we emphasize close horizontal relationships with each other.[16] Congregations need to be structured so that both the large group and the small groups can be vital.

While the church after Constantine emphasized only the large church, the Anabaptists out of necessity experienced the church primarily in the context of small groups. As a result, they were shaped as much by their form as by their theology. Leaders like Menno Simons helped join the small groups into networks. Most healthy congregations today are networks of healthy small groups.[15]

If the church is where we give and receive counsel, we can do that best in small groups. If the church is where we experience fellowship and encouragement, we can also do that best in communities of 12 or less where we know each other well. If the church is where we discern each other's gifts or work together in service projects, we also do that best in small, Christ-centered communities. Some would say that the small group, rather than the congregation, needs to be seen as the basic unit of the church. Anabaptist-minded Christians will likely see:

1. Forgiveness as vital to community.
2. The community as necessary for the interpretation of Scripture.
3. Small groups as essential to the life of the church.

Christ-centered community is the center of our life! Are you an Anabaptist-minded Christian?

Core Value #3: Reconciliation is the center of our work

For the early Christians, being a Christian was a blend of *believing* in Jesus, *belonging* to the church, and *behaving* in a new way.[17]

Jesus

Jesus came so that people might believe, become part of God's family, and be empowered to behave in a new way. The early disciples helped many throughout the known world to become reconciled to God and to each other. Jesus anticipated that people would offend each other in this new family so he provided steps for reconciliation as outlined in Matthew 18. Offended persons are to go to each other one-to-one. If the offense is not resolved, further steps are to be taken.

In the Sermon on the Mount (Matthew 5-7), Jesus gave guidelines for behavior in God's family. He taught his disciples that true peace comes through knowing the truth, repenting of wrong, and treating people in a new spirit. "Don't just love those who love you," he commanded. "Even the pagans do that much! Love your enemies and pray for those who persecute you" (Matthew 5:43-48).

At the end of his ministry, Jesus said, "As the Father has sent me, so send I you" (John 20:21). "Go into all the world and make disciples of all peoples, baptizing them and teaching them to obey everything that I have commanded you" (Matthew 28:18-20).

One of the greatest challenges facing the early Christians was the racial, religious and cultural conflicts between Jews and Gentiles. After ministering to people of many backgrounds, and inviting many into the family of God, the Apostles were reconciled and came to agreement on how people from these different backgrounds could become one body through faith in Christ. As a result, the church developed a culture of peace.

Early believers were transformed in their thoughts, relationships and actions. This happened through belief in Jesus, belonging to each other in small groups, and through the power of the Holy Spirit. For the first 250 years, they refused to engage in military combat. They understood that they were under orders to love their enemies, not kill them. Jesus had taught them to pray for those who persecuted them and to overcome evil with good.

The Apostle Paul saw the first Christians as ambassadors of reconciliation and said, "All this is from God, who reconciled us to himself through Christ and gave us the ministry of reconciliation" (2 Corinthians 5:18). If you would have asked those first Christians, I believe they would have said, "*Reconciling people to God and to each other is the center of our work!*"

Constantine

Unfortunately, Constantine and Augustine did not continue in this tradition. While **Constantine** affirmed Christianity and took Christian priests into his ranks, he did not make a major change in his beliefs, belonging or behavior. Constantine marched entire armies through the river to baptize them even though many, and probably most, had not been changed in their beliefs, relationships and style of life. Instead of seeking to reconcile people to God and to each other, he was intent on conquering them for political gain.

Augustine

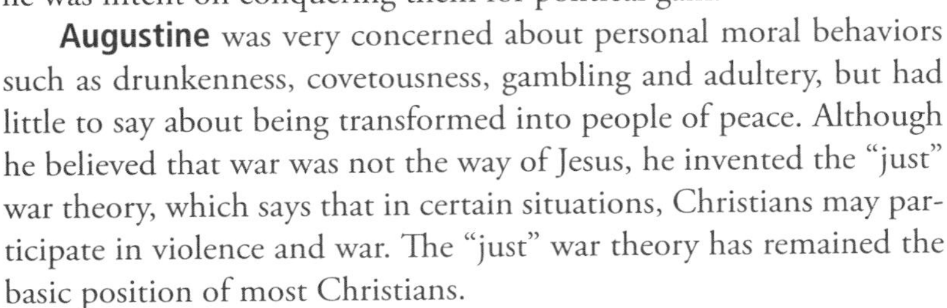
Augustine was very concerned about personal moral behaviors such as drunkenness, covetousness, gambling and adultery, but had little to say about being transformed into people of peace. Although he believed that war was not the way of Jesus, he invented the "just" war theory, which says that in certain situations, Christians may participate in violence and war. The "just" war theory has remained the basic position of most Christians.

Martin Luther

Theologically, **Luther**, Zwingli, Calvin and others followed in Augustine's footsteps. They emphasized personal forgiveness, obedience to the Ten Commandments, and accepted the "just" war theory. Although some new understanding of faith had been accomplished, these mainline reformers fell short of seeing the church radically changed. Unfortunately, the difference between the behavior of Christians and non-Christians became almost indistinguishable.

Early Anabaptist Christians under the leadership of Menno Simons and others believed that through a personal relationship with Christ and obedience within a Spirit-filled community, a person's behavior could be changed into the likeness of Christ. They emphasized peace with God, peace with each other, and peace with their enemies whom they refused to fight. The Sword of the Spirit, the Scriptures, was their only weapon.

In its own way, the Anabaptist movement was the charismatic or Holy Spirit movement of the 16th century.[18] Anabaptist leaders spoke more about the Holy Spirit than did the other reformers. They believed that the Holy Spirit empowered them for evangelism and caused new believers to change their behavior.

The Anabaptist movement was also the evangelistic movement of the Reformation. With evangelistic passion, key leaders went throughout Europe seeking to reconcile people to God and to each other.[19] By the thousands, people joined this new movement.

The Anabaptist movement was also a movement for social justice. Their leaders addressed many of the economic and social concerns held by peasants who were revolting against the dictatorial nature of the feudal system.[20] As a result, the movement gained many members from among the peasants, who then gathered into small congregations throughout much of Europe.

Through their study of Scripture and their emphasis on transformation of life, most Anabaptist Christians came to believe that it was wrong to participate in war and violent behavior. Like the early disciples, they refused to join the military even though the enemies of Western civilization were at the gates of Vienna. Rather than fight back against their persecutors, they chose to follow the example of Jesus who "did not retaliate when people hurled their insults at him, and made no threats when he suffered" (1 Peter 2:23).

Menno Simons

If you would have asked them, I believe that **Menno Simons** and most of these early Anabaptist Christians would have said with the early disciples, "*Reconciling people to God and to each other is the center of our work!*"

Anabaptist-minded Christians today are guided in their work by three specific concepts:

1. Accepting Jesus leads to transformed living

Anabaptist-minded Christians believe that to be a Christian one needs to believe in Jesus, belong to his body, and behave in a Christ-like manner. This is only possible when we have been renewed by the Holy Spirit through the transformation of our minds and hearts.

Just as God took the initiative in Jesus Christ to reconcile us to himself and to invite us into his family, so we are to take the initiative to share the gospel with others so that they might be reconciled to God, adopted into his family, and transformed in their lifestyle. We are to continually look for opportunities to invite people to accept Jesus as their Savior and Lord so that this might happen.

We become Christians when we "surrender as much of ourselves as we can to as much of Christ as we can understand."[21] Accepting Jesus will cause us to change our thinking, our friendships, and our way of living. Broken or alienated people will be transformed as they join us in God's family where we, too, are being transformed. The new relationships and context change nearly everything and bring us together into a stark contrast with the world. Mental, emotional, physical and social areas of life are transformed through our new relationships with Christ and each other.

2. Transformed people "think reconciliation"

Transformed people "think reconciliation" and involve themselves in ministries of reconciliation. While some Christians believe that evangelism is at the center of their work, others emphasize peace and social action as their center. These two important parts of outreach can be brought together in the concept of reconciliation. The purposes of God are "to reconcile to himself (God) all things through Christ" (Colossians 1:19).

When we come upon someone who is in conflict with God, with a neighbor, a fellow employee or a family member, we are not to immediately denounce one party or take sides. We are to "think reconciliation." This may mean exploring the cause of the conflict and helping the parties to make it right through honest confession, careful listening, unselfish forgiving, and appropriate restitution.

Anabaptist-minded Christians feel called to help people of all backgrounds, genders, races and nations into a relationship with Christ and with each other. Solving problems and reconciling relationships is at the center of our work. However, we need to remind ourselves that we cannot help others to go farther than we ourselves have gone. Even as we seek to help others become transformed, we need to keep growing in our own understanding of how we need to be changed.

3. Transformed people work for peace

As transformed followers of Jesus, we are to fight evil as hard, or even harder, than anyone else. But we need to fight differently. Jesus used words, emotions and nonviolent actions, not guns and bombs. At all times, we are called to imitate the example and spirit of Jesus. The Sermon on the Mount gives us guidance. The Holy Spirit gives us the power to live in this highly disciplined way. Our "attitude should be the same as that of Christ Jesus" (Philippians 2:5). We are challenged to say with the Apostle Paul, "For though we live in the world, we do not wage war as the world does. The weapons we fight with are not the weapons of the world" (2 Corinthians 10:3-4).

It is due to our view of salvation as transformation that Anabaptist-minded Christians refuse to be involved in war and violence. While modern warfare teaches soldiers to lie, to hate and to destroy, those whose minds and spirits have been transformed by Jesus will refuse to do such things even if commanded to do so by important authorities.

History and experience indicate that violence leads to more violence. Violence can only be reduced by nonviolence and by correcting the injustices that motivate it.

Unfortunately, millions of people have died and are still dying because Christians, in the tradition of Constantine, Augustine and Luther, are involving themselves in war instead of serving as reconcilers. As followers of Christ, we need to give ourselves to loving our enemies, praying for those who persecute us, and to overcoming evil, "'not by might nor by power, but by my Spirit,' says the Lord Almighty" (Zechariah 4:6). In summary, Anabaptist Christians believe that:

1. Conversion leads to transformed living.
2. They are to "think reconciliation."
3. They are to work for peace in all areas of life.

Reconciliation is at the center of their work. Are you an Anabaptist-minded Christian?

Conclusion

What are we to think of the Anabaptist understanding of the Christian faith? It has been said that the great principles of freedom of conscience, separation of church and state, and voluntarism in religion so essential to democracy are derived from the Anabaptists of the Reformation period. They clearly enunciated them and challenged the Christian world to follow them in practice.[22]

What is an Anabaptist Christian? I have attempted to clearly state the core values of Christian faith from an Anabaptist perspective. The problem of Christianity is not necessarily its many denominations, but rather the hesitancy of its parts to learn from each other. Anabaptist Christians have much to learn from Christians of other cultures and traditions in regard to such matters as the sovereignty and grace of God, the importance of the creeds, and the methods of participating in government. Christians of other backgrounds may also have much to learn from the Anabaptist tradition on such matters as following Jesus in daily life, interpreting the Scriptures from a Christ-centered point of view, and giving primacy to the Lordship of Christ.

Do the following statements summarize your understandings of the Christian faith? If they do, you are an Anabaptist-minded Christian.

Jesus is the center of my faith.

__ I fix my eyes on Jesus, the author and perfector of my faith.
__ I interpret the Scriptures from a Christocentric point of view.
__ I seek to follow Jesus in daily life. Christianity is discipleship.

Community is the center of my life.

__ I believe forgiveness makes community possible.
__ I study the Scriptures with others to discern their applications for our time.
__ I affirm that small groups are basic to a healthy church.

Reconciliation is the center of my work.

__ I am called to help reconcile people to God through faith in Jesus.
__ I believe evangelism and peacemaking come together in reconciliation.
__ I reject all forms of violence and encourage peaceful alternatives to war and other forms of conflict.

Endnotes

1. Jack Trout, *Differentiate or Die* (New York: John Wiley and Sons, 2000).
2. James C. Collins and Jerry I. Porras, "Building Your Company's Vision," in *Harvard Business Review* (Lewes, Del.: Harvard Business Publishing, September 1996).
3. This alliteration of values is adapted from Grace Davie by Alan Kreider in his book, *The Change of Conversion and the Origin of Christendom* (Eugene, Ore.: Wipf and Stock Publishers, 1999), pp. xiv–xvi.
4. Harold S. Bender, *The Anabaptist Vision* (Scottdale, Pa.: Herald Press, 1944).
5. For a well-researched study of the changes to the process of incorporating new believers into church membership, see *ibid.*, Alan Kreider, *The Change of Conversion.*
6. For a biography of Constantine, see William Smith, ed., *A Dictionary of Christian Biography,* Vol. 1 (New York: AMS Press, 1974), pp. 623-649.
7. For an outline of Augustine's life and theology, see Erwin Fahlbusch, ed., *The Encyclopedia of Christianity,* Vol. 1 (Grand Rapids, Mich.: Eerdmans Publishing, 1999), pp. 159-165.
8. John D. Roth, *Stories: How Mennonites Came to Be* (Scottdale, Pa.: Herald Press, 2006). See chapter 2 for descriptions of the revolt, reform, and renewal of the Reformation.
9. For further understanding on the various streams of Anabaptism, see C. Arnold Snyder, *Anabaptist History and Theology* (Kitchener, Ont.: Pandora Press, 1997).
10. See *Anabaptism in Outline*, edited by Walter Klaassen (Scottdale, Pa.: Herald Press, 1981) for primary sources related to themes that were important to the Anabaptists.
11. *Ibid.*, pp. 23-24, 72-73 and 140ff.
12. Peter Kehler was a colleague in mission. He served in Taiwan from 1959-1975 and 1991-1993.
13. For more on the theme of political involvement, see John H. Redekop, *Politics Under God* (Scottdale, Pa.: Herald Press, 2007).
14. John D. Roth, *Stories: How Mennonites Came to Be* (Scottdale, Pa.: Herald Press, 2006), chapter 4.
15. William A. Beckham, *The Second Reformation: Reshaping the Church for the 21st Century* (Houston, Tex.: Touch Outreach Ministries, 1998), pp. 25-26.

16. Palmer Becker, *Called to Care and Called to Equip* (Scottdale, Pa.: Herald Press, 1993).
17. *Ibid.*, Alan Kreider, *The Change of Conversion*, pp. xiv–xvi.
18. Walter Klaassen, *Living at the End of the Ages* (Lanham, Md.: University Press of America, 1992), chapter 6, "The Age of the Spirit."
19. Hyoung Min Kim, *Sixteenth-Century Anabaptist Evangelism* (Ann Arbor, Mich.: ProQuest, 2002).
20. For contemporary application of how discipleship relates to issues of justice and social action, see Ronald J. Sider, *I Am Not a Social Activist* (Scottdale, Pa.: Herald Press, 2008).
21. Samuel Shoemaker, *How to Become a Christian* (New York, N.Y.: Harper and Row, 1953), p. 71.
22. *The Recovery of the Anabaptist Vision*, edited by Guy F. Hershberger (Scottdale, Pa.: Herald Press, 1957), pp. 29-30. This volume also includes a wealth of essays on the rise and theology of Anabaptism.

Perspectives and questions for discussion

Core Value #1:
Jesus is the center of our faith

Fix your eyes on Jesus, the author and perfector of our faith.
(Hebrews 12:2)

Many Christians emphasize:

1. Christ's death
Many Christians focus on the holiness of God and their need for justification. They emphasize the death and ressurection of Christ without a proper emphasis on the life and teachings of Jesus. Christianity is forgiveness.

2. A "flat" Bible
Many Christians tend to see the Scriptures rather than Jesus as their final authority. Guidance for daily living comes from various Scriptures that seem to fit the situation. All decisions do not need to coincide with the teachings and spirit of Jesus.

3. Government as final authority
Many Christians believe that since government leaders are ordained of God, they must be obeyed even if their demands are contrary to the teachings of Jesus or the dictates of their conscience.

Anabaptist Christians emphasize:

1. Christ's life
Anabaptist Christians affirm the holiness and forgiving grace of God, but also give strong emphasis to the transforming power of the words, ministry, and spiritual presence of Jesus. Christianity is discipleship.

Do you agree with the statement, "Christianity is discipleship?"

2. A "Christ centered" Bible
Anabaptists affirm that all Scripture is inspired, but that Jesus is the fullest revelation of God. He is the final authority for decision-making. Jesus fulfills the Old Testament and is the norm for both personal and social ethics.

Explain the difference between a "flat" and a "Christ-centered" Bible.

3. Jesus as final authority
Anabaptists recognize that government is ordained of God and must be obeyed insofar as obedience to Christ will allow. However, the demands of government shall not overrule the Lordship of Jesus.

What does it mean for you to say, "Jesus is Lord?"

Core Value #2: Community is the center of our lives

Every day …
they broke bread in their homes
and ate together with glad and sincere hearts,
praising God and enjoying the favor of all the people.
(Acts 2:46-47)

Many Christians emphasize:

1. Vertical forgiveness
Many Christians focus more on vertical forgiveness from God than on horizontal forgiveness with each other. Forgiveness is seen as a means for receiving individual salvation and eternal life.

2. Individual interpretation
Just as the medieval church insisted that only church leaders were capable of correctly interpreting the Scriptures, many Christians rely almost totally on trained teachers or pastors to tell them what a Scripture means.

3. Meet in sanctuaries
Many Christians tend to think of the worshiping congregation as the basic unit of the church. Too often, the church is seen as a structure, an organization, or as a Sunday morning performance.

Anabaptist Christians emphasize:

1. Horizontal forgiveness
Christians need both vertical forgiveness from God and horizontal forgiveness from each other. Forgiveness is a means to community, to peaceful relationships with each other.

How does forgiveness contribute to community?

2. Corporate interpretation
Anabaptist believe that individual study of Scripture must be combined with group study. Group members commit themselves to giving and receiving counsel in the spirit of Jesus.

In what ways do you study the Bible together in your church?

3. Meet in small groups
Anabaptist Christians see the church as a family. Many healthy churches are organized as networks of small groups in which members fellowship, study, share and pray together.

Are small groups basic to the life of a healthy church? If so, how might they become a greater reality in your congregation?